Kate Calder

Illustrated by Bonna Rouse

Crabtree Publishing Company

www.crabtreebooks.com

Created by Bobbie Kalman

For Joel Vsetula

Editor-in-Chief
Bobbie Kalman

Author
Kate Calder

Managing editor
Lynda Hale

Editors
Niki Walker
Amanda Bishop
Heather Fitzpatrick
Hannelore Sotzek

Computer design
Lynda Hale
Kate Calder

Photo researcher
Kate Calder

Production coordinator
Hannelore Sotzek

Special thanks to
Marie-Christine Turineck, Dr. David Turineck, John Siemens, Katherine Siemens, Stacey Wallace, Adele Thomson

Photographs
Bruce Curtis: pages 3, 8 (top), 9 (bottom), 10 (both), 11 (both), 12, 13 (bottom), 16, 21 (top left and right), 22, 23 (both), 24 (bottom), 25 (both), 29, 30, 31 (right); Bob Langrish: front cover; John Siemens: back cover; SportsChrome: page 31 (left); Kim Stallknecht/SportsChrome: page 5; Diane Thomson: title page, pages 4, 6-7, 8 (bottom), 9 (top), 13 (top left and right), 15, 17 (all), 18, 19 (all), 20, 21 (bottom), 24 (top), 26

Illustrations
All by Bonna Rouse except: David Calder: page 28; Tammy Everts: page 11

Digital prepress
Embassy Graphics

Printer
Worzalla Publishing Company

Every reasonable effort has been made in obtaining authorization, where necessary, to publish images of the athletes who appear in this book. The publishers would be pleased to have any oversights or omissions brought to their attention so that they may be corrected for subsequent printings.

Crabtree Publishing Company
www.crabtreebooks.com 1-800-387-7650

PMB 16A
350 Fifth Avenue,
Suite 3308
New York, NY
10118

612 Welland Avenue
St. Catharines,
Ontario
Canada
L2M 5V6

73 Lime Walk
Headington,
Oxford
OX3 7AD
United Kingdom

Cataloging-in-Publication Data
Calder, Kate
Horseback riding in action

p. cm. — (Sports in action)
Includes index.

ISBN 0-7787-0167-0 (library bound) — ISBN 0-7787- 0179-4 (pbk.)
This book introduces the techniques, equipment, and safety requirements of horseback riding as well as caring for horses.

1. Horsemanship—Juvenile literature. [1. Horsemanship.] I. Rouse, Bonna, ill. II. Title. III. Series: Kalman, Bobbie. Sports in action.

SF309.2 .C36 2001 j798.2'3—dc21 LC 00-057077
CIP

Contents

What is Horseback Riding?

Horseback riding is a sport in which a rider and horse work together to perform in contests of skill and endurance. The sport includes riding over **jumps** and through a series of difficult **maneuvers** with perfect technique. Horseback riding has many other purposes as well. Some people ride horses to help them carry out tasks on farms and ranches. Many ride for fun and recreation on trails. Horses are also used in rodeos, racing, and acrobatic stunts, known as **vaulting**.

What are Equestrian Events?

"**Equestrian**" describes events related to horseback riding. Riders learn how to move their body in order to direct their horse around obstacles and over jumps. Learning how to control a horse takes many hours of practice and hard work. To test their skills, riders enter local, national, and international competitions. Some even compete in the Olympics.

English and western

There are two styles of riding—English and western. Ranch workers use **western-style riding** to drive cattle over miles of pasture. Rodeo competitors also ride western style. **English-style riding** is used for equestrian events and general purpose riding. The English saddle is smaller than the western saddle. English-style riders hold the **reins** with two hands and they **post** during a trot (see page 22). This book describes horseback riding as it is done using an English saddle.

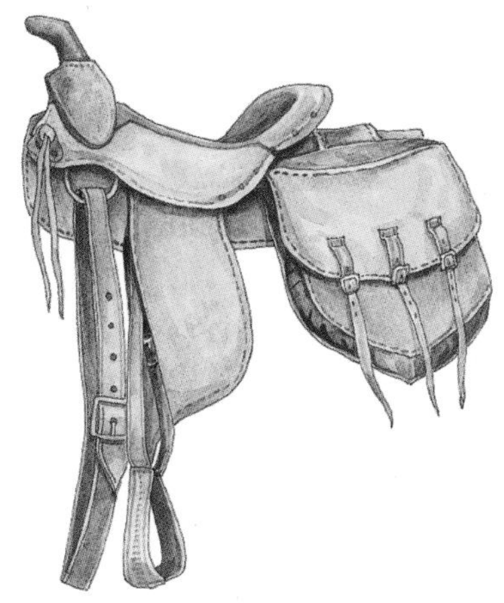

A western-style saddle has a high back and a horn at the front for attaching rope. To guide the horse, riders hold the reins with one hand. The rider above has to hold the reins with both hands to get his horse under control.

All About Horses

Besides having a distinct personality, each horse has a different **conformation**, or overall body shape. Becoming familiar with your horse and its body will make learning to ride easier. Study the horse's body on these pages to help you understand the riding lessons that follow later in the book.

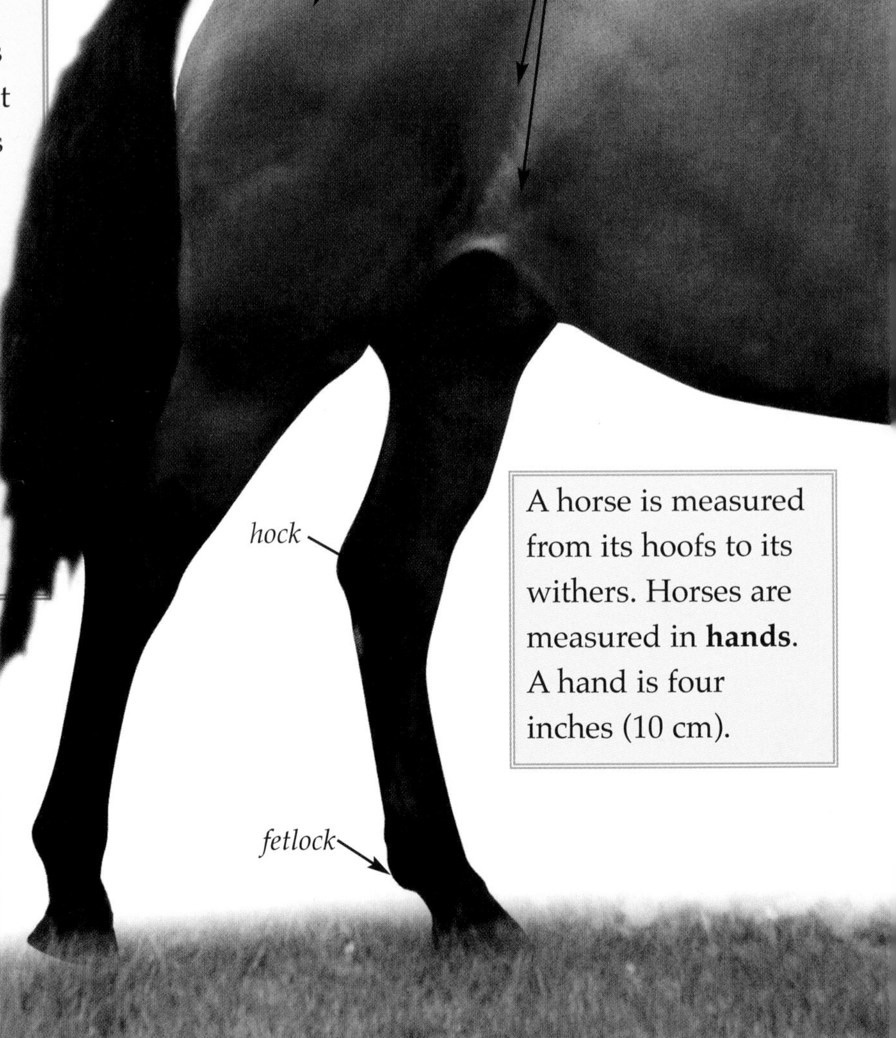

Horse power

Horseback riding began as a means of transportation. Horses have great strength and stamina, which means that they can pull or carry loads over long distances without getting tired. For hundreds of years, people relied on horses to get them from place to place. Horses were also used in the military. Military officers held competitions to test their jumping and riding skills.

A horse is measured from its hoofs to its withers. Horses are measured in **hands**. A hand is four inches (10 cm).

Hoofs are made of **keratin**, which is the same material as that found in your fingernails.

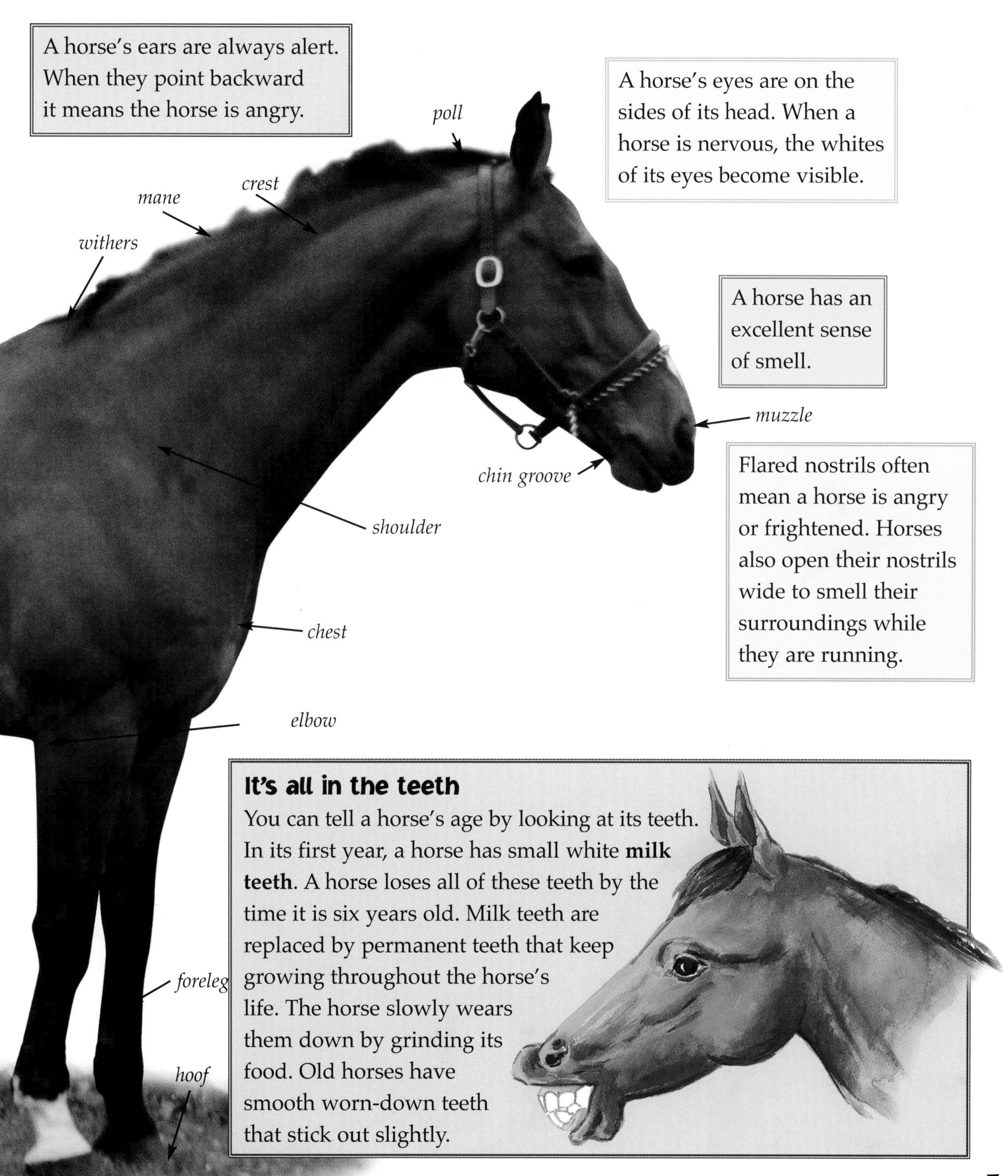

A horse's ears are always alert. When they point backward it means the horse is angry.

A horse's eyes are on the sides of its head. When a horse is nervous, the whites of its eyes become visible.

A horse has an excellent sense of smell.

Flared nostrils often mean a horse is angry or frightened. Horses also open their nostrils wide to smell their surroundings while they are running.

It's all in the teeth

You can tell a horse's age by looking at its teeth. In its first year, a horse has small white **milk teeth**. A horse loses all of these teeth by the time it is six years old. Milk teeth are replaced by permanent teeth that keep growing throughout the horse's life. The horse slowly wears them down by grinding its food. Old horses have smooth worn-down teeth that stick out slightly.

Caring for Horses

Having a horse may be fun, but it is also a lot of work! You must be sure to give your horse fresh food and water several times a day. Its stall must be cleaned out and lined with fresh bedding such as straw or wood shavings at least once each day. You also have to exercise your horse to keep it healthy. Giving your horse plenty of attention will keep it happy.

(left) This horse is wearing a ***flymask*** *to keep pesky flies from flying around its eyes. The horse can see through the flymask.*

Horse food

Grazing, or nibbling on grass, is the natural way for horses to get food. In the winter, when grass does not grow, horses are fed hay. They may also be fed grains such as oats, barley, corn, or linseed, depending on the job they do for their owner. Horses must have a supply of clean water at all times.

Mucking out

Cleaning, or **mucking out**, your horse's stall every day is essential. Use a pitchfork to remove the dirty straw and droppings. Lay fresh straw in the stall. The straw should be at least four inches (10 cm) deep. You can use wood shavings instead of straw. Wood shavings do not need to be replaced as often, but you still have to remove the droppings and soiled shavings every day.

Horse health

It is important to pay attention to your horse and watch for signs of sickness. A healthy horse has a smooth, shiny coat, bright eyes, and alert ears. A sick horse may not want to eat or drink. The horse may have difficulty breathing or be moist with sweat. If your horse limps, its foot or leg could be **lame**, or injured. Pebbles in the bottom of a horse's hoof can cause lameness. Keep a journal of your horse's symptoms and visits from the vet to help you monitor your horse's health.

(above) This rider is using a pitchfork that rakes through the bedding to pick up the droppings.
(below) This horse is having its legs soothed in a whirlpool made especially for horses.

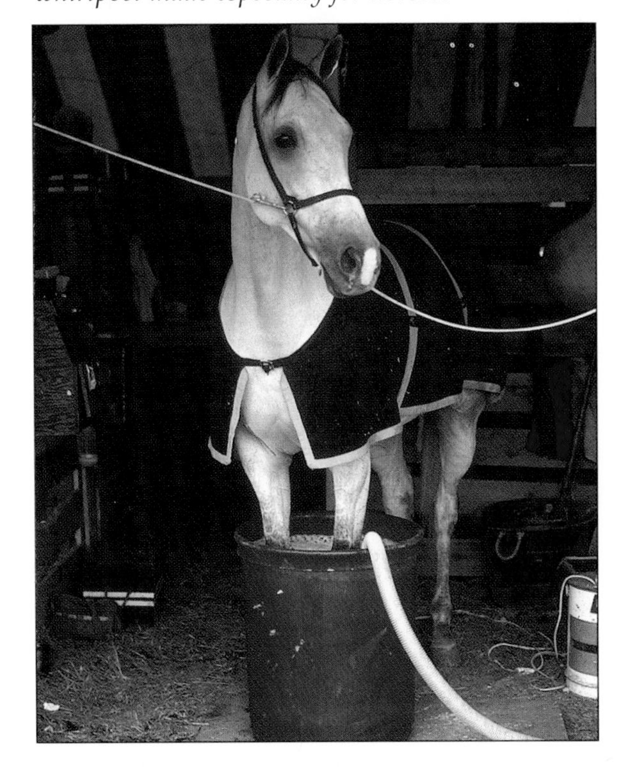

Grooming

It is important to keep your horse clean. Not only will your horse look good, it will stay healthier, too. When you **groom**, or clean, your horse, you remove dirt, sweat, and grease from its coat. You also remove small bugs that can infect your horse's skin. As you rub your horse's coat, you are massaging its muscles and helping blood flow through its whole body.

Carry your grooming supplies neatly in a wooden box like the one above. How many kinds of brushes do you see in this box?

Start with a brush

You will need several brushes for grooming your horse. A **dandy brush** has long, wiry bristles for removing dirt and sweat. With a **body brush**, use long strokes to smooth the horse's coat from head to tail. Brush the same direction in which the hair grows. Use a **mane comb** to separate tangles in the mane and tail.

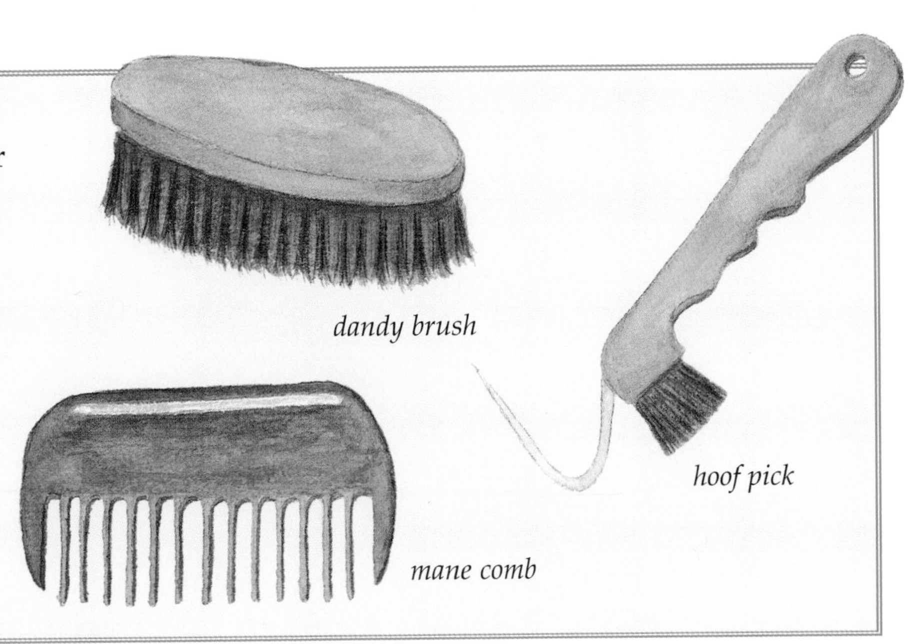

Foot care

Use a **hoof pick** to keep hoofs free of pebbles and large chunks of dirt that could injure your horse. Brush the top of the hoofs with **hoof oil** to keep them from drying and cracking.

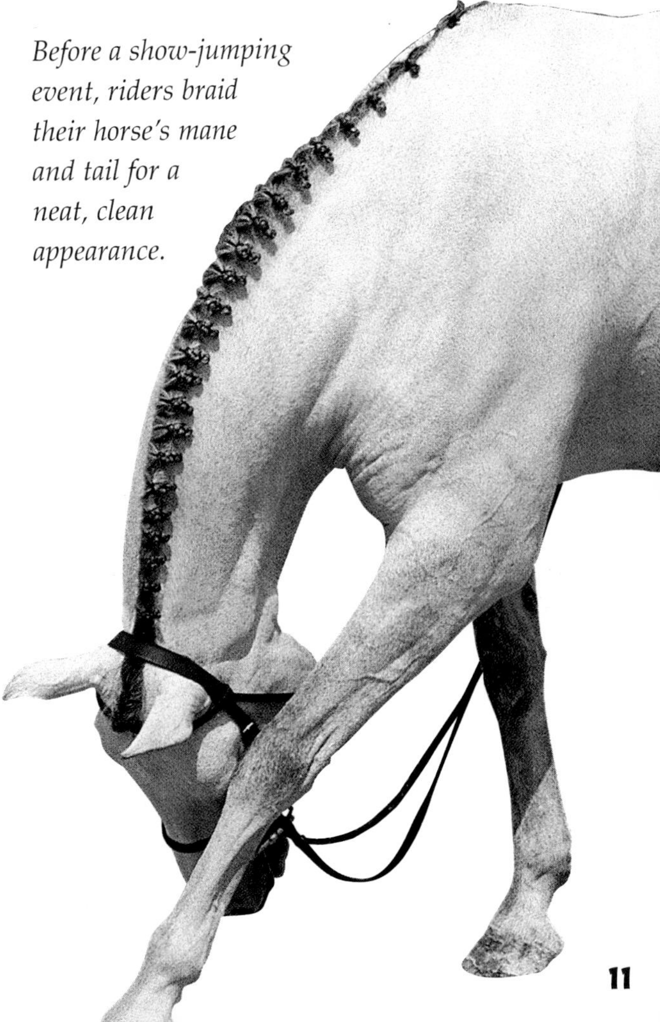

Before a show-jumping event, riders braid their horse's mane and tail for a neat, clean appearance.

Essentials

Before you can ride your horse, you need to outfit it with some equipment. Riding equipment is called **tack**. It includes gear such as a **saddle** and **bridle**. There is also gear that you need to wear. During equestrian competitions, you will wear clothing such as the outfit shown on the left.

Riders wear a **riding hat** with a chin strap to protect their head.

Gloves help the rider keep a secure grip on the reins.

Riding pants, called **jodhpurs**, have patches on the inside of the legs to keep the material from wearing out.

Most riders wear tall boots. Small heels keep the rider's foot from slipping through the **stirrup**.

Strap on a seat

A saddle is a seat that allows you to sit securely and comfortably on your horse's back. It also keeps you on the proper spot so that you do not hurt the horse's spine. A saddle is a wood and metal frame that is covered with padding and leather.

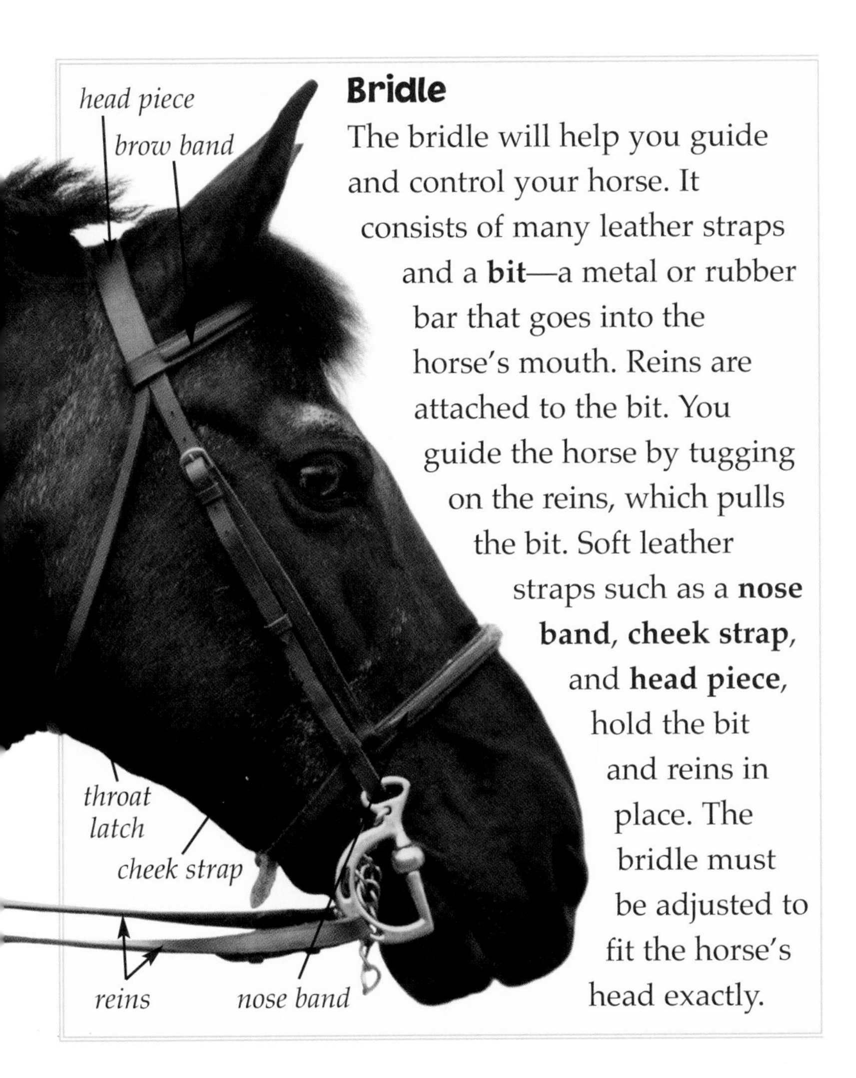

Bridle

The bridle will help you guide and control your horse. It consists of many leather straps and a **bit**—a metal or rubber bar that goes into the horse's mouth. Reins are attached to the bit. You guide the horse by tugging on the reins, which pulls the bit. Soft leather straps such as a **nose band**, **cheek strap**, and **head piece**, hold the bit and reins in place. The bridle must be adjusted to fit the horse's head exactly.

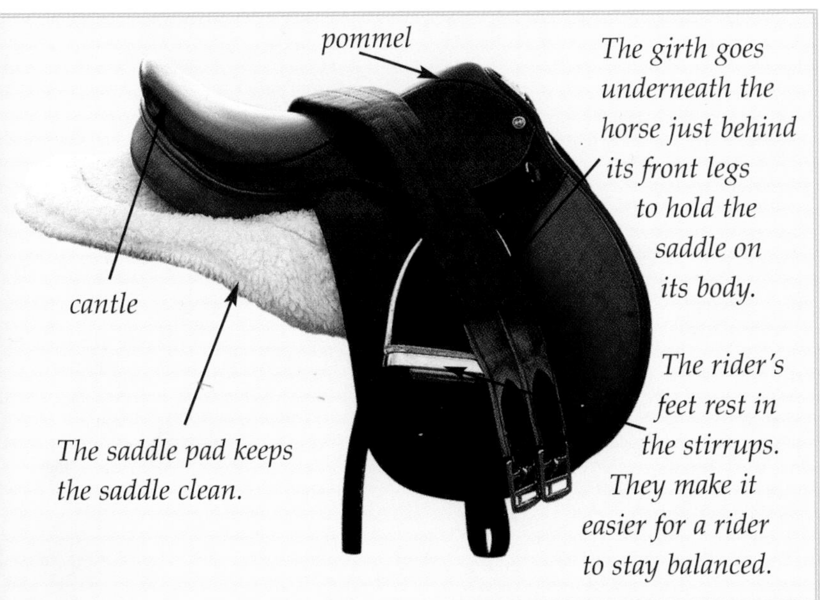

The girth goes underneath the horse just behind its front legs to hold the saddle on its body.

The saddle pad keeps the saddle clean.

The rider's feet rest in the stirrups. They make it easier for a rider to stay balanced.

Room and board

Many horse owners do not own a stable in which to keep their horse. They **board** and care for their horse at a **boarding stable**.

Riding schools

You can take private or group riding lessons. If you do not have a horse of your own, you do not need to worry. Most beginners do not own a horse. Many riding schools provide horses for the students to ride.

Getting Ready

Before you ride, you need to stretch and warm up your muscles. Warming up will prevent your muscles from becoming pulled or strained. Stretching also helps your body relax. A horse can tell when you are tense or uncomfortable, and it will become nervous, too. Spend a few moments stroking and talking to your horse to help it relax. A relaxed horse is easier to control than a nervous one.

Do the twist

Stand with your feet shoulder-width apart and your arms outstretched. Twist your upper body to one side and then the other. Repeat ten times.

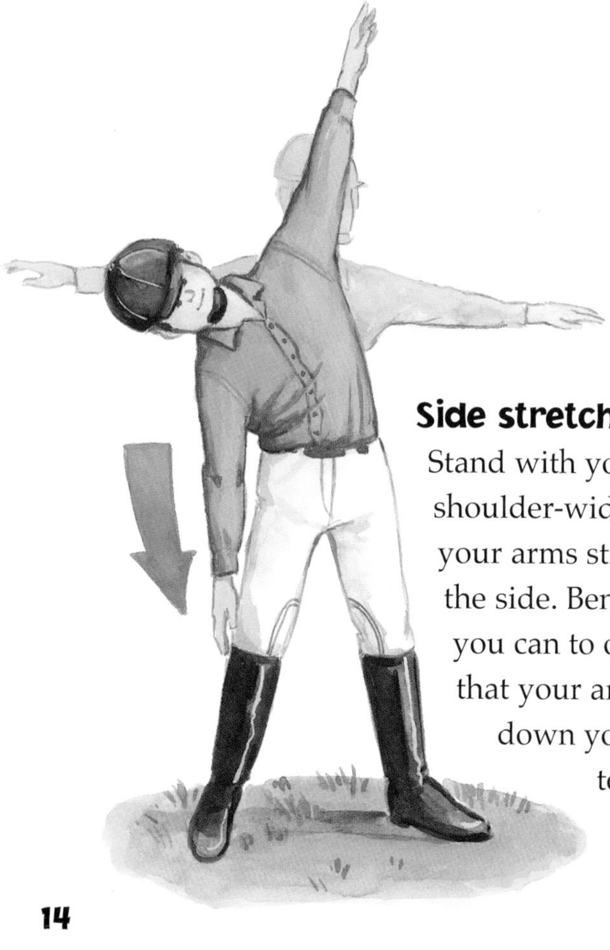

Side stretch

Stand with your feet shoulder-width apart and your arms straight out to the side. Bend as far as you can to one side so that your arm slides down your leg. Bend to the other side and repeat ten times.

Leg swing

Standing straight and using a chair for balance, swing one leg back and forth ten times. Keep the knee of your swinging leg slightly bent. Repeat the swings with the other leg.

Approach with caution

Horses do not like loud noises or quick movements. Move close to a horse with your shoulder facing the horse's shoulder so that it can see you clearly. As you move around a horse, gently touch it to let it know exactly where you are at all times.

Danger zone

Never stand directly behind a horse—it could easily kick you! When you move toward the back of the horse, keep touching it and talking softly so that the horse knows where you are. Sudden movements or sounds may startle the horse and cause it to kick.

When you first approach your horse in the stall or field, move slowly from the front or side while speaking in a soft voice. Hold the ***halter*** *in one hand behind your back. With the other hand, hold out a carrot or an apple as a treat to encourage the horse to let you approach.*

On and Off

Before you **mount**, or get on, your horse, you have to know how to put on a saddle. The saddle must fit snugly so that it will not slip to the side. First, place the saddle flat on the horse's back. Next, reach under its belly and grab the girth strap. Tighten the girth strap gently under the horse's elbows. Make sure the horse's skin under the strap is not pinched. Adjust the stirrups so that they hang an arm's length from the saddle. Remember to hold onto the reins to keep control of the horse in case it moves forward.

How to mount:

Stand on the left side of the horse. Hold the reins in your left hand on top of the horse's shoulder. If you are not tall enough to reach the stirrup, stand on a mounting box.

Place your left foot in the stirrup. With your right hand, grab the back of the saddle. Hold onto the mane gently with your left hand. Lean forward and pull yourself up.

Spring up and swing your right leg over the horse's back. Lower yourself gently into a sitting position in the saddle. Put your right foot in the stirrup.

Dismounting

When you are ready to get off your horse, ask your instructor or a partner to hold it steady. First, take both feet out of the stirrups. Lean forward and swing your right leg over the back of the saddle. Never swing your legs in front of you to dismount. You could fall backward if the horse moves suddenly. Keep your body facing the horse's body and drop slowly to the ground. Hold the reins snugly in case the horse moves forward while you dismount.

In the Saddle

The first step to riding well is developing an **independent seat**. Having an independent seat means you are able to balance securely and comfortably on the horse without using the reins. The exercises on the next page will help you develop a good independent seat. Ask someone to hold your horse while you practice these moves.

You should be able to sit in the saddle with your shoulders and legs relaxed and your back straight.

Leg raises

Take your feet out of the stirrups and raise them to the sides. Hold your arms out as well.

Lean back

With your feet in the stirrups, lean back as far as you can while keeping your legs straight down.

Stand up

Stand in the stirrups with your weight on your heels. Raise your arms to shoulder height and balance in the standing position.

Touch your toes

Reach for your right foot with your left hand. You will need to lean forward and across the horse.

Basic Moves

Once you are comfortable sitting on the horse, you will be ready to ride as it walks. You have to communicate with the horse to make it move. Signals that tell the horse when and how to move are called **aids**. Your hands, legs, voice, **seat**, or the way you sit in the saddle, and your weight are all aids that allow you to guide the horse.

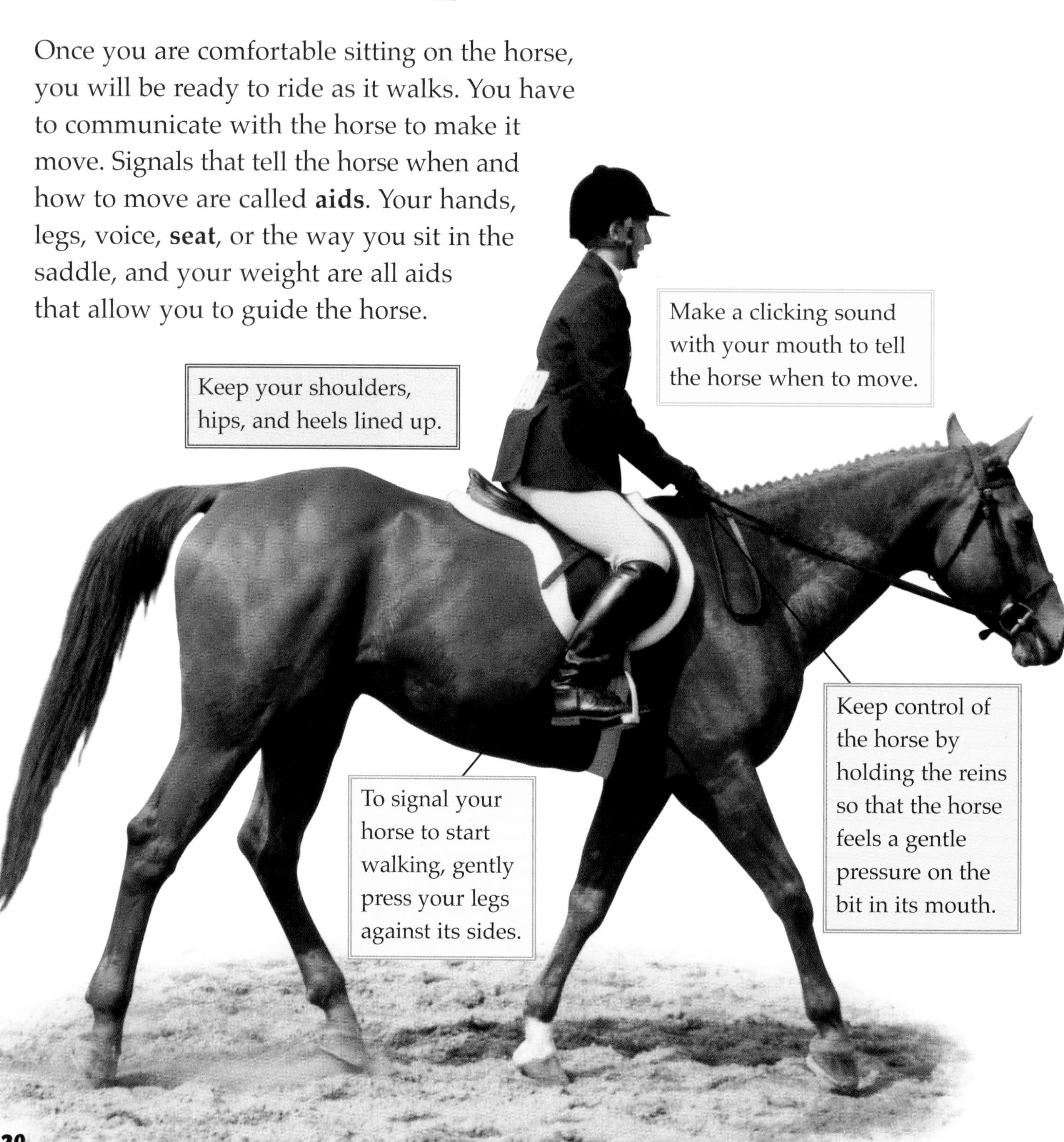

Artificial aids

Hands, legs, seat, weight, and voice are called **natural aids** because they are parts of the rider which help control the horse. **Artificial aids** are devices such as a **whip**, shown right, and **spurs**, shown below. Aids are not used to hurt the horse but to urge it to move. A rider taps the horse on its rear to urge it forward.

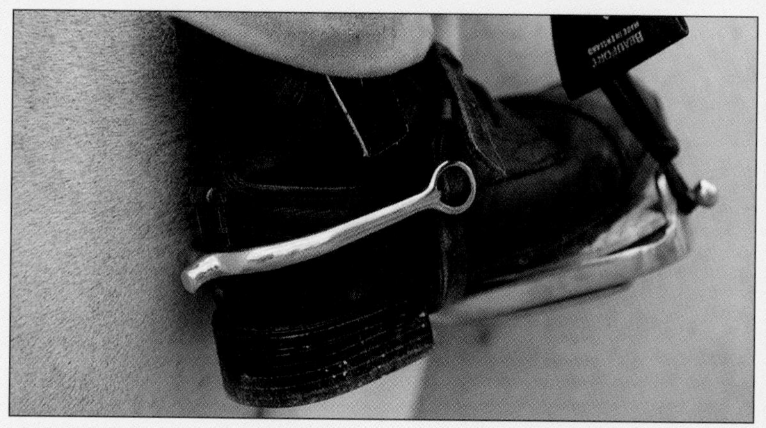

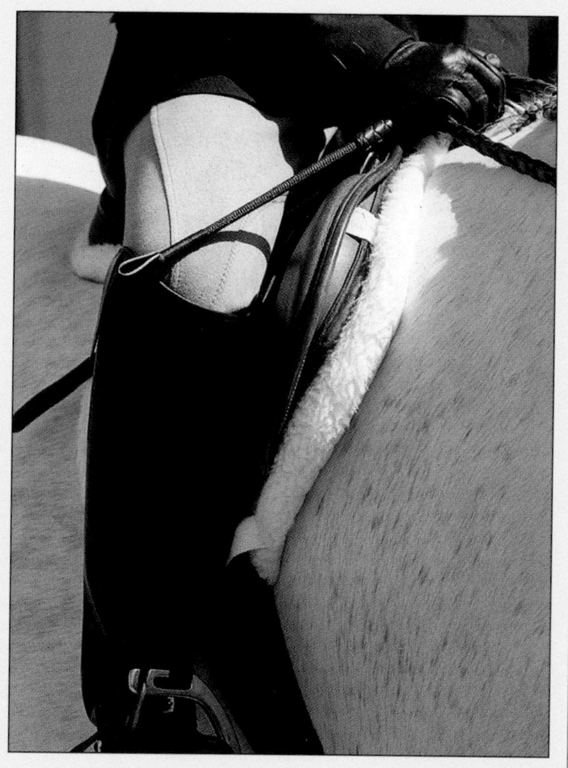

Turning

Your legs are important aids for turning. To turn right, press your leg against the horse's right side. Move your left leg back to keep the horse's rear from swinging out too far. Use your hands to guide the horse by pulling lightly on the right rein. The rider on the right is looking at the direction in which she wants to go to help guide her horse around a curve.

Stopping

To stop, gently increase pressure on both reins at the same time. Keep your shoulders, hips, and heels in a straight line and let your weight sink into the saddle. You can say "whoa" to let the horse know that you want it to stop.

Giddy-up

Horses move at different paces called **gaits**. **Walking**, **trotting**, **cantering**, and **galloping** are common gaits. Switching from one gait to another is called a **transition**. A rider uses aids to signal the horse to make a transition.

You will feel a front-to-back rocking motion when the horse canters. Try to sit firmly in the saddle and let your hips move with the motion.

Trotting away

A trot is a slow, bouncy gait. To go from a walk to a trot, squeeze the horse's sides with your legs. You may have to tap the horse gently with your heels to encourage it to move. Riders post, or rise themselves up and down, as their horse trots. The rider goes up on the first beat of the trot and down on the second.

As a horse canters, it stretches one front leg farther forward than the other. The horse's diagonal legs move together during a canter.

Trot to canter

The canter is a fast, bounding pace. The horse starts a canter with its back leg. You must signal to the horse to let it know with which back leg to **strike off**, or take the first step into the canter. Keep your inside leg at the girth of the saddle and squeeze your opposite leg behind the girth. Gently put pressure on the inside rein and then release it as soon as the horse begins to canter.

The gallop

The gallop is a horse's fastest gait. The horse stretches out all its legs in a running stride. To make the transition from a canter to a gallop, squeeze the horse's sides with the lower part of your legs. During a gallop, sit in the **forward seat** position. To sit in the forward seat position, bring your seat out of the saddle, bend forward slightly at the waist, and keep your balance over the center of the horse. Let your hands allow the motion of the horse's neck to move freely.

Keep light pressure on the reins so you can indicate to the horse to slow down at any time if it starts galloping too quickly.

Jumping

Jumping requires a lot of practice and courage from both the horse and the rider. Beginners should always learn to jump on an experienced horse and with the help of an instructor. The instructor should teach you the body positions and aids that will encourage your horse to jump. You must be totally ready as your horse approaches a jump. If not, the horse will sense your hesitation and stop short. The sudden stop can cause you to fall.

Walk your horse over poles laid on the ground and spaced evenly. Next, trot over the poles to get a feel for going over jumps. Practice leaning forward as you go over the poles.

This rider is jumping for the first time. To achieve better balance, she should not lean so far forward.

Steps to jumping

The five steps to jumping are the **approach**, the **take off**, the **moment of suspension**, the **landing**, and the **getaway**. Doing each step properly is important in jumping safely.

1. Approach

As you and your horse approach the jump, look straight ahead and lean forward slightly.

2. Take off

Move your legs slightly back and begin squeezing them against the horse's sides. Relax at the waist and shift your weight forward.

3. Moment of Suspension

Balance your weight over the front of the horse (shown top, right) and lift your seat out of the saddle. Let you arms follow the horse's neck movement forward and down.

4. Landing

As your horse lands, softly return to the saddle. Bring your body back to an upright position (shown right.)

5. Getaway

Maintain your balance and posture as you ride away from the jump.

Keeping Control

Horses are nervous animals that often make quick, jumpy movements. Be aware of things in your surroundings that could startle your horse. Loud noises, sudden movements, and flashes of light can make a horse **deke,** or change direction suddenly, causing you to fall off. When your horse acts jumpy, stay calm. Panicking or losing your temper will only make the horse more upset.

When a horse sees a sudden movement or flash, it may ***shy****, or jump away. A pole on this jump fell and scared the horse, causing it to refuse to jump.*

Rearing

Sometimes your horse will **rear**, or raise itself up on its hind legs (shown right). Rearing is scary and difficult to control. If your horse rears, lean forward and try not to pull on the reins. Beginners should not ride horses that are known to rear.

Nappy behavior

Horses can be **nappy**, or stubborn. Your horse may try to turn around or swing in a different direction than where you want it to go. Sometimes, it may try to go back to the stable! Use the reins to guide your horse back on track. Apply stronger leg pressure to urge it forward. Use your voice and your whip to encourage the horse.

Graceful falling

Sometimes riders cannot avoid being thrown off their horse. Knowing how to fall properly will help keep you from getting hurt. The most important thing to remember is to relax your body as you fall. If possible, curl your body to protect your arms, legs, and head and then roll away.

Horse Shows

Competing in horse shows tests a horse's skill and endurance and the rider's ability to control and maneuver the horse. Riders of all levels compete in different events at horse shows.

Show jumping

In **show jumping**, the horse and rider demonstrate their jumping and riding abilities on a course. The course has several obstacles, over which the horse jumps in a set order. The jumps look solid, but they are made up of loose pieces that will fall easily if knocked.

Each time a horse knocks down an obstacle, it adds a **fault**. The rider who directs a horse around the course in the shortest time, and with the fewest faults, wins.

Hunter

In a **hunter event**, the riders focus on executing the jumps with perfect technique rather than trying to complete the course in the shortest amount of time. The winners show the best form while jumping the fences and keeping the best pace and stride between them.

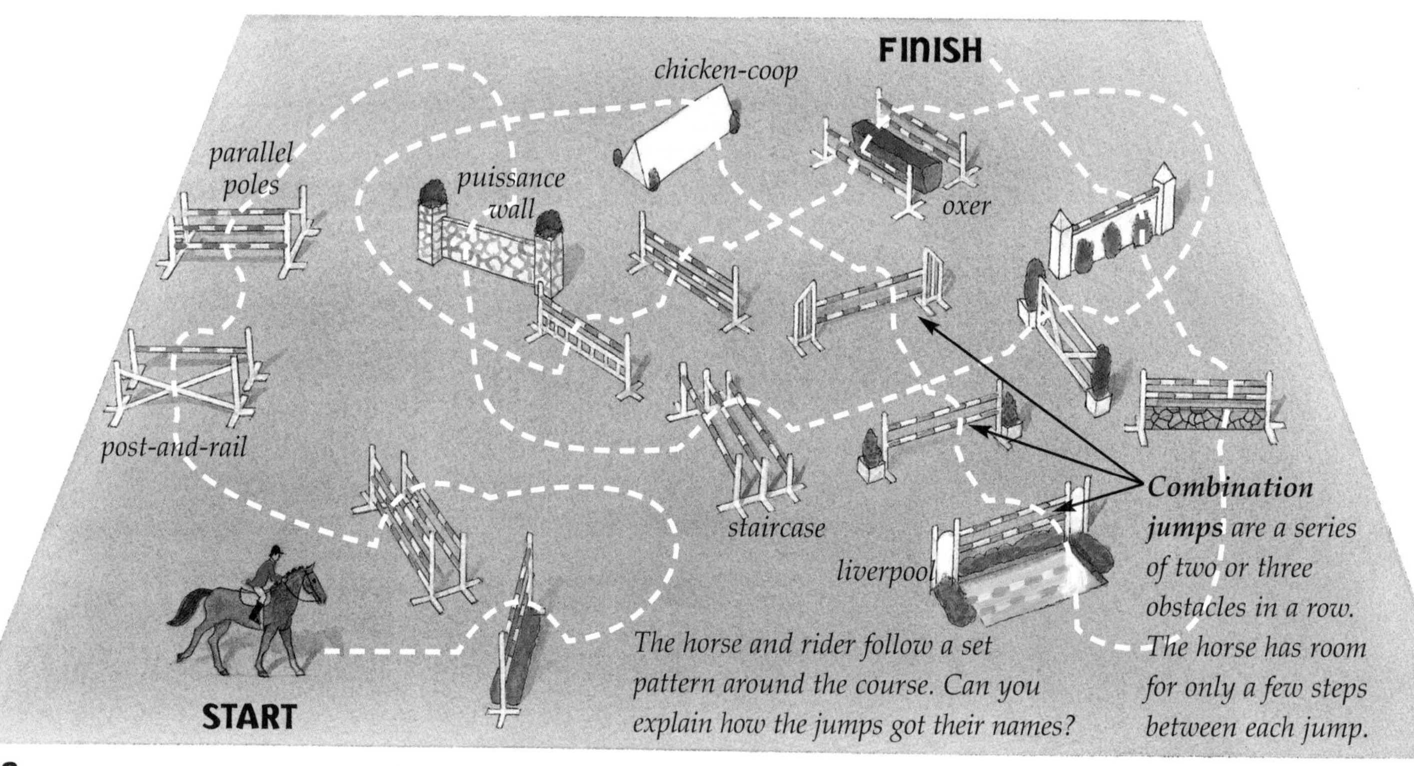

The horse and rider follow a set pattern around the course. Can you explain how the jumps got their names?

***Combination jumps** are a series of two or three obstacles in a row. The horse has room for only a few steps between each jump.*

Speed and endurance

Only experienced riders take part in the **speed and endurance event**. The horse and rider travel several miles over country trails, roads, and hills. One phase of the event, called the **steeplechase**, is a two mile (3 km) course with difficult jumps. Horses take off or land on uneven ground. The speed and endurance event takes a lot of skill. Some of the jumps land in water.

(right) ***Cross country*** *is an event in which riders race over three to five miles (5 to 8 km) of open land and jump over obstacles.*
(below) This rider is competing in a show jumping event. He is jumping over parallel poles.

Equitation

Many horse show events test a rider's skill in **equitation**. Equitation is the skill with which a horse and rider perform their maneuvers. Riders are not concerned with speed but rather with form and appearance. Judges look for perfect technique as the horses and riders move through their paces.

In **flat-class events**, a horse and rider execute different gaits. The rider tries to demonstrate perfect form as he or she guides the horse through walking, trotting, and cantering as well as changing directions. The rider who shows the best form and control over his or her horse wins.

Dressage

Dressage is an event in which the rider guides the horse through a series of intricate and complicated movements such as the **half-pass** and the **pirouette**. The rider uses small precise movements with his or her hands and legs as aids to guide the horse. Performing dressage movements shows off a rider's control and a horse's skills and obedience. Riders at all levels can compete in dressage events. The levels range from beginner to the most advanced, known as **grand prix**.

(left) Both men and women in high levels of dressage riding wear a long, black tailcoat, a white shirt, tall black boots, and a top hat.

(above) Riders win different colored ribbons for placing first, second, or third.

Riding Words

board To pay a stable in exchange for keeping and taking care of a horse
conformation The overall build and appearance of a horse
dressage The discipline of training a horse to perform maneuvers with slight leg, hand, and weight movements
gait The pace at which a horse moves, such as walking, trotting, cantering, and galloping
half-pass A dressage movement in which the horse moves forward and sideways
halter A device made of straps that fits on a horse's head and is used to lead it.
hoof pick A tool with a metal pick used to remove stones and grit from hoofs
independent seat The ability to balance firmly on a horse without relying on use of the rein or the stirrups
maneuver A movement or procedure involving skill and control
pirouette A dressage movement in which the horse turns on one spot
post To rise up and down out of the saddle in rhythm with the horse's gait
steeplechase A horse race over rough land with hedges and ditches over which to jump

Index

1 2 3 4 5 6 7 8 9 0 Printed in the U.S.A. 9 8 7 6 5 4 3 2 1 0